STRONG HELP
FOR
STRONG MEN

By

Daynel W Collins

ISBN: 1-4107-7806-1 (e-book)
ISBN: 1-4107-7807-X (Paperback)

Library of Cnogress Control Number:
2003095914

This book is printed on acid free paper.

Printed in the United States of America
Bloomington, IN

1stBooks – rev. 08/07/03

Acknowledgements

Lord, I first have to tell you thank you for allowing me to have a beautiful life in you, I also want to thank you for your direction and your purpose. Mom, thank you for being a great mother, because; you are excellent one. Aunt Carol, Roslynn, and Stephanie thank you for encouraging me to write. Aunt Carol see I write my goals. Roslynn, I love you, keep being you. Stephanie, you are very special there is something great waiting in life for you. To my beautiful sister Lynnette you always will be my beautiful role model. To my sweet Diamonte' you are my first baby and know matter where I go you are with me. Daddy, you have been a catalyst for most things positive in my life and I love you. Little Glenn, I love you too. Hettie's Hearts, I love you. To all the men I love you and God love you he is always blessing you. To all the people on this page and all the people who are not, I love you and God is blessing you.

Sincerely,

Daynel

Dedication

Lord, I have written this book in faith and obedience to you. Every page is to honor you and give you glory so I dedicate it to you, along with my life.

Preface

Dear, Readers

I wrote this book through the inspiration of two scripture Genesis 1:27 and Genesis 2:18. I want to see all people, especially; men become self-sufficient in there faith by knowing love, being somebody in love, and being outrageously powerful because of love.

This book is designed to make you feel much stronger through three main subjects love, image and biblical education.

The first chapter is on love and a pure definition of love. How it can make are life worth living, the myths that people believe about love, its beauty and strength.

The second chapter is on image no matter what it is positive or negative that it can still not be beneficially in your life and people are suppose to help you with finding a proper image but if they don't you can still get yours in line. Lining your image up affects you and future generations.

The last chapter is on biblical education, which unlocks life possibilities by empowering you and making a you self-sufficient Christian.

Your Helper

Daynel

Table of Contents

The Power Move

LOVE:

The Real Deal

Daynel W. Collins

LOVE: The Real Deal

In our society, we well know that there are many misconceptions. The major one is on love. To achieve and maintain anything you must have a clear definition of what it is. It is important so you can know how it functions and what to do to maintain its function. Having a lack of education or no education on the subject of love cause us a great deal of error in our relationships. The problem comes from misunderstanding of what love is. Therefore, we usually end up destroying our relationship because we confuse a lot of different terms and concepts with love. The major terms that are confused with love are relationship, respect, and sex. Confusing love with these terms cause us to be disrespectful and disrespected all in the name of what we considers love. Our definitions are not clear and vary person-to-person and relationship-to-relationship. Some believe if you base love on trust, communication and reciprocation it will work and it will last but this is a lie. The major reason it is confusing is because it is different for each person and is not clearly defined.

However, the bible has the real deal or genuine definition. The bible lays it out real plain in 1 John 4:16 AMP, "And we know (understand, recognize, are conscious of, by observation and by experience) and believe (adhere to and put faith in and rely on) the love God cherishes for us. God is love, and he who dwells and continues in God, and God dwells and continues in him". The bible definition of love is God. This bible verse actually defines love in equal terms as God making the word love and God interchangeable. Meaning that wherever you see the name of God you should be able to replace it with the word love, and wherever you see the word love you should be able to replace it with the name of God.

This scripture also tells you how to achieve and maintain love. It is through dwelling and continuing to dwell in God. Better put in our common language is to live and continue to live in God. To live in God is to have an acceptance of his son's Jesus Christ, his life, burial, and resurrection or in plain terms salvation. To have salvation is achievement of a relationship with love. This achievement is something that can never be taking away from you. Salvation is the beginning of living in God and God living in you. Maintaining this relationship is to grow and mature in God or to allow God to grow and mature in you. This is, why the scripture says, "continue in God, and God dwells and continues in him" meaning to go forward in God or love and allowing God to do the same in you. To do this you must understand how God is. There is a clear description of this found in the bible 1 Corinthians 13:4-7 AMP "Love endures long and is patient and kind; love never is envious nor boils over with jealousy, is not boastful or vainglorious, does

7

not display itself haughtily. It is not conceited (arrogant and inflated with pride); it is not rude (unmannerly) and does not act unbecomingly. Love (God's love in us) does not insist on its own right or its own way, for it is not self-seeking; it is not touchy or fretful or resentful; it takes no account of the evil done to it [it pays no attention to a suffered wrong]. It does not rejoice at injustice and unrighteousness, but rejoices when right and truth prevail. Love bears up under anything and everything that comes, is every ready to believe the best of every person, its hope are fadeless under all circumstances, and it endures everything [without weaking]".

This is a description of how God is a standard of things that he always does or never will do. To continue in God or love you must also live by these standards. Continuing may seem so hard but it easier than you think. It is easy to keep the standard of love due to the first scripture given 1 John 4:16. Remember, that God in you wants to grow.

So, when you don't understand or are disobedient to God's he will teach you or correct you. In Proverbs 3:12 AMP it states, "For whom the Lord loves He corrects, even as a father corrects the son in whom he delights". This scripture says that he corrects us but is also implies teaching. Since, a father who corrects a son is trying to show him the right things to do. It is important too distinguish the difference between correcting and teaching. Correcting comes when you are deliberately or directly disobedient to what you know is correct. Being corrected for disobedience may come in many different unpleasant forms. Usually it is the conviction of the action of your disobedience emotional, physically, mentally and or spiritually. Think about one of your sins you committed when you were directly disobedient. Emotionally, the thing you did made you feel a little depressed. It probably had a physical consequence whether you tried to acknowledge it or not. If you're honest with yourself, you will admit that you spent time thinking why did I do that? Last, you probably felt so bad about it you didn't feel that you could talk to God about it. However, God was working it out through all those feelings. This is why we should limit our acts of direct disobedience so we can enjoy God. He wants to grow in us even when we sometimes don't want to grow. Disobedience hinders the enjoyment of love. Disobedience hinders are enjoyment of love and slows down our growth process. We should also be careful of disobedience and loving God in lip service because of how he considers obedience to him. He actually accredits obedience as an act of love towards him. In John 14:15 AMP it states plainly, "If you [really] love Me, you will keep (obey) My commands." He wants this obedience in three specific areas. These areas are laid out in the Deuteronomy 6:5 ICB, "Love the Lord your God with all your heart, soul and strength." According to this scripture, the heart is your motive. The soul is your mind, which is gives you the ability to educate yourself. Strength is how you conduct yourself through your actions. Your motive is the reason why you do things. If it is not being done to uplift the teachings of Christ, help yourself or others come closer to Christ and or please God in the process it should not be done. Our motive is what God measures. He talks about this when he chose David to be his king in 1 Samuel 16:7 NIV, "But the Lord said unto Samuel, Do not consider his appearance or his height, for I have rejected him. The Lord does not look at the things man look at. Man looks at the outward appearance, but the Lord look at the heart." The roles you take in life must also please God roles as husband, businessman, father, friend, and etc. This is where educating yourself in the word of God comes in. That is the second area of obedience your soul or mind that is to be scholarly or act as a student of the word trying to learn what the bible says and means. So, you know what God says about those roles. Your mind or soul is built up through what you put in it. It is like your body; it is built up through your diet. When you put the proper kind of food and beverages in your body the healthier it is or becomes. This process is the same when it comes to your soul or mind. Inputting scriptures, stories and sermons help make you a stronger Christian. The last area is your strength or actions, which help you, follow through on your motive and mind. Doing and being obedient to what you have learned. When you build your mind or soul it helps you to know what to do. It gives you deliberate steps to take for any situation you are involved in work, marriage, divorce, sexuality, and all that could arise good or bad.

Now, teaching occurs when you don't know and God shows you what is correct. God teaches us just how the scripture say in 1 John 4:16 he will bring it to our attention. He will allow you to recognize it through observation in someone else's life. He may speak to you directly through the Holy Spirit. The sermon of the week may be on this particular sin. When you read your bible or other materials God will show you that what you have done is not correct. He will also show you how to avoid it next time. This teaching is also preparation for things to come in your life. Just like any other education that prepares for your future. Teaching and correcting are big part of continuing in God, and not as hard, as you think once you are aware that this is what is happening in your life.

Since, you now have a clear definition of love. You need to re-educate yourself on the things that our often confused with love or considered love like the terms relationship, respect, and sex. Relationships, respect and sex are confused with love because they are part of love but not God. They are vessels, instruments and tools to enhance the distribution of love in our lives, but not love.

A relationship is a connection to you, others, and or an organization through your thought feelings and or actions. For example, connecting to yourself would be doing self-esteem drills. Looking in the mirror saying I am a beautiful person inside and out. Connecting yourself with others would be example of, relationships were you would go places with people and have conversations and share like interest with one or more persons. When you have a relationship with an organization or activity. You would be doing things such as, going to work, joining a church choir or just singing in the shower all these are relationships. A relationship is having a connection with a person, place or thing with your thoughts, feelings or actions. Having a relationship is a normal everyday occurrence, but it is not love.

It is a tool that God uses to allow love to flow through evenly and generously in our lives. An example of this is how a lamp uses electricity to omit light. What you need to know is that electricity itself is never the problem. It is the outlet, electrical device, wiring but never electricity. Just like love if there is a malfunction in our relationships, we can never blame it on love. We need to find out what is wrong with the relationship and fix it. You cannot allow the damage in you relationships to go unfixed because it may cause needless damage or death to the relationship. You need to find out if it is you or the other human being. Is it the difference of ideals, it is repairable or do you have to scrap the whole relationship. The key to knowing whether it is repairable or whether it needs to be thrown away is if it can keep the standards of love that are laid out in 1

Corinthians 13:4-7. Without following these standards, you are disrespecting Love. Which leaves your relationship running at dysfunctional. Many people who are in serious long-term relationships try to make their relationships functions. They try everything they know how sex, vacations, children, therapy, church, prayer, and money. Many Christians don't know that their relationships must show the glory of God. Relationships are vessels that allow us to help build each other up through conversations and actions that should be centered on God. The problems arise when the focus is put directly on the two vessels instead of on God. When we allow God to be the binder and filter for our relationships according to his holy word are relationships will work properly. They will work like a lamp plug into a light socket. A relationship without love is not worth keeping.

Many people mistake relationship for love because they can bring items such as joy, peace, strength things that are involved in love. Then even when these things start to dissipate we allow ourselves to hold on to relationships. That lead us to disrespect others, God and ourselves. Using all types of excusing to maintain these relationships no matter what the cost. Excuses like the length of time together, secrets shared and arrange of excuses. The whole time God is saying, "I am love. I have loved you and if this relationship disrespects me it need to be over. If this relationship will not move back to place of obedience in me, scrap it. I have loved you before you were a glimmer in your father's eye, or smirk on your mother's lips. I know all your secrets and all your excuses get focused on me and I will repair your broken heart, I am love." Love is God, not a relationship so don't allow your self to be disrespectful and disrespected to keep a relationship because you have mistaken it for love. A relationship is a vessel of love and it is a vessel that can take on different shapes, and can be broken beyond repair.

Respect is another tool; it is a tool to enhance the distribution of love in our lives. Clarity of this word is important because many our starting to use this word for a substitution for the word love. In today's society, the term self-respect is being used to build a generation of people up and/or down. Respect is honoring, valuing, and appreciating you, someone or something. It is holding you, someone, or something else in a select and special group.

The problem with respect it has the ability to change. The things that people respect vary person-to-person, issue-to-issue and situation-to-situation. It leaves out commitment, and it can rapidly grow into pride. Respect can do this since it focuses on human wants and desires not on God's will. Being in pride distorts our judgment it cause most people to do the wrong things for the right reasons or do the right things for the wrong reason. Pride is simple not putting Gods desire first. Seeking a direction or a path he has not purposed for you. No, matter how profitable it is or seems to be. Many people have an appreciation of college and or university education, which is wonderful. However, if this is not the path that God has sent you on it is pride. There are two simple scriptures that talk about the difference between what paths too chose and why. Proverbs 15:24 AMP states, "The path of the wise leads upward to life, that he may avoid [the gloom] in the depths of Sheol (Hades, the place of the dead)." The other is Proverbs 14:12 AMP it states, "There is a way which seems right to a man and appears straight before him, but at the end it is the way to death." These Proverbs both talk about paths one that is correct and one that seems right and leads to death or hell. Doing what seems right is not acceptable if it contradicts what God wants you to do.

Whether, it is what parents, family, friends or society respects we have a responsibility to God to find out what his path is for our life. Respecting someone or something beyond God's will is dangerous.

Keeping away from over stepping things you respect or simple put walking in pride to keep away from doing this it is done in two ways praying and researching Gods word. We need to pray because many people fall into pride by doing the wrong thing and trying to fix them in there will and not God's. An example, of this is a person who gets married because; they have had a child outside of marriage. Compounding sin covering an unacceptable sexual act and joining in union that God has not prearranged for you. Basing your actions on what seems right instead of repenting and trying to find out what is next in God planned for your life. Keep in mind that God is love and the road of pride is destruction. In this example, the parents are caught in a unhappy marriage based on commitment instead of love. The child that they got married for suffers wondering who or what love is. This is an example of many decisions that people make that seem right. Doing what seems right not only affects you but also affects others around you. God uses what he creates to bless this world and you are apart of it. However, if you are doing good things and not God's thing you are hindering your blessings and other people too. Just as the example above. The father and mother of one child make significant impact on a person life by doing what God wills not what seems right. This is the same for every individual in society who does what God wills not what seems right. There are many people in the bible who broke the respect of there family, friends, and mores of society to receive the blessing of God's will. Jesus on more that several occasions broke many religious rules healing on the Sabbath, befriending a prostitute and a crooked cop (a tax-collector) to name only a few things. Ruth had to leave her family to get to her blessing. David a shepherd became king and Esther a poor girl became queen following God's will not what seemed right. The bible is filled with people who did not except there own desire or what they respected but became great through doing what God had purposed for them.

There is a danger in our society with the word respect, self-esteem, and self-respect these words are overrated and overused by us, on our children, family and friends. We must be sure that these words are being used properly.

Basically, we need to make sure we are not shunning people by saying that they don't have these things. We also need to make sure when these traits are accredited to us we have acceptable response. Making sure that we give God proper credit for what he has done for us. There are many scriptures, that deal with this form of pride and it is boasting. Taking on the credit for abilities, gifts, skills, or opportunities that God has given us. Our society is filled with messages that tell us to do just that boast in ourselves. Not in the fact, that God has provide brain function, breathing, and aptitude and all other life. In 2 Corinthians 10: 17-18 AMP it talks about proper boasting. "However, let him who boasts and glories boast and glory in the Lord. For [it is] no [the man] who praises and commends himself who is approved and accepted, but [it is the person] whom the Lord accredits and commends." He has provided everything.

The last reason respect needs to be looked at thoroughly is because it is involved in one of the deepest relationship in our society, marriage. The bible ask men to love there wives in Ephesians 5:33 AMP "However, let each man of you [without exception] love his wife as [being in a sense] his very own self; and let the wife see that she respects and reverences her husband [that she notices him, regards him, honors him, prefers him, venerates, and esteems him; and that she defers to him, praise him and loves and admires him exceedingly]." This request seems simple but if you don't know the difference between love and respect it is not simple. Respect is what he asks women to do for there husbands. It is also laid out in this scripture. So, respecting someone is noticing them, holding them in high regard, honoring them, preferring them, giving them venerates, esteeming them giving them praise holding them in a place of high appreciation. Many men hold us women at places of high value by buying us the best of things, taking us to the best of places. However, you don't love us by laying down your life for us treating us the way that you want to be treated. Laying down your life means both in the physical unto death and it also means to change or give up your life for the betterment of your marriage. Many of you cheat and know that this is not something you want done to yourself, are abuse, or act like tyrants and stead of loving. Even when you cheat you still hold your wife in place of greater appreciation than the person your cheating with. You would never allow another person to overshadow the place of respect that you have put your wife in. For some women a place of respect is enough because it leaves her with an upper hand. Feeling disrespected because she has caught you cheating is to her advantage. Some, women will make you pay to level of respect that they feel was damaged. There first demand will be ending the relationships with the person or thing that has caused the disrespect. Then there will be variations of other paybacks whether it is taking and dealing with her poor attitude. This is the worse because it will probably never end. Then there are women who just want things monetary gifts, sex, vacations, and all your attention. Once they feel you have paid your way out and they are restored to their place of respect the cycle will start again until one of you get tried of this cycle. Most women don't realize that this is what is going on so don't get mad at her when you read this. This cycle occurs due to lack of education on what love and respect are and human nature not game playing. So, if one or both of you get a comprehension of Ephesians 5:33. That the husband is supposed to love the wife not just respect her. Once again love is God. To act like God goes back to 1 Corinthians 13:4-7 those standards are how you are suppose treat your wife. It also means that you are suppose to treat her how you want to be treated and how God treats the church. That may take some minor research however being respected by her is probably worth it. You need to remember when you only respect your wife and not love her this is being disobedient and prideful. By, walking outside of the will of God for your life and your marriage and family.

Respect can be the start of love or pride. Depending on whether you will be at God's will and give him credit for his will or be at your own will and take credit for his will, grace, and mercy. Pride is destructive and God's will is prosperous without hurt a complete blessing. When you walk outside of pride and do what God ask and not all the things you respect it allows you to be free from feeling the burdens of mistakes. You can have peace because you are not responsible for the success or failures of your whole life. Just the failures that you know you know you made because you decide to do things your way not God's way.

Having a respect for things is important because it is the step before love. However, respecting things beyond their proper use is a major problem. When you seek to respect morality, education, beauty, sex, power, marriages, relationships, heritage, children, money and etc beyond the purpose given to them by God there becomes a problem. The problem is that you never fully enjoy these things because you always use them improperly and you usually damage yourself or others with them. You are willing to give them up easily, or misuse them to gain something else. Respect is not bad. However, we as Christians have to make sure that what we respect God respects, in the same context of use.

This leads to something that God respects, but is often misused, sex. It is often misused because it is misunderstood seeing that it is the most taboo word in the church. It is not a subject that the ministries address well they don't educate people. The most people know about sex is that is not for people who are not married to each other or not married. There is so much more to this subject and that is what people need to hear. They need to hear the biblically facts, about what sex does, what benefit it plays in marriage and what disadvantages it creates when it is done outside of marriage. Sex is often perceived as love because these two terms are not defined and we are not told the effects they have on our lives from the biblically perspective. Sex, is a tool that enhances love in our lives after marriage. The purpose of this tool is to unite a married couple. It causes the couple two form a unique bond of oneness emotionally and spiritually. In Genesis 2:24NIV, "For this reason a man will leave his father and mother and be united to his wife, and they will become one flesh." Since, sex is usually missed used and oneness is created between individuals that are not supposed to be together forever and are not suppose to have a spiritual and emotionally connection. The connection that is created is mistaken for love and this cause people to stay in relationships that are unhealthy, abusive, dangerous and deadly. It also leads people to marry the wrong people, not get married at all or see love as the blame for heartache. If you spend time being guide by a false love in different relationships sexual or non-sexual. You are not going to be in the right places and doing the things that God has planned or purposed for you. You can only be lead by one thing at time. Being lead by love is life filled with beautiful relationships, purpose, and wonderful blessings. However, when something is mistaken for love it will begin to take the place of God and lead you toward destruction.

That is why love can never be mistaken for sex, respect or a relationship.

Love is God and not anything else. He is genuine, real; limitless he has been and always will continue to be the same. He remains himself even when we change and are disrespectful, unaware, and or rebelliously sinful. When we are not being ourselves or when we are acting typical of our personality, he never ever changes. The Psalmist David talks about this unchanging love in Psalm 139:1-18 NIV "O Lord, you have searched me and you know me. You know when I sit and when I rise; you perceive my thought afar. You discern my going out and coming and my lying down; you

are familiar of all my ways. Before a word is on

my tongue, you know it completely, O Lord.

You hem me in-behind and before; you have

laid your hand upon me. Such knowledge is too

wonderful for me, too lofty for me to attain.

Where can I go from your Spirit? Where can I

flee from your presence? If I go up to the

heavens, you are there; if I make my bed in the

depths, you are there. If I on the wings of the

dawn, if I settle on the far side of the sea, even

there your hand will guide me, your right hand

will hold me fast. If I say, "Surely the darkness

hide me and the light become night around me,

"even the darkness will not be dark to you; the night will shine as light to you. For you are created my inmost being; you knit me together in my mother's womb. I praise you because I am fearfully and wonderfully made; your works are wonderful, I know that full well. My frame was not hidden from you when I was made in the secret place. When I was woven together in the depths of the earth, your eyes saw mine unformed body. All the days ordained for me were written in your book before one of them came to be. How precious to me are your thoughts, O God! How vast is the sum of them! Were I count them; they would outnumber the grains of sand. When I awake, I am still with you."

This Psalm articulates that God has been and always will be love. It sums up everything in the chapter that I have been writing trying to say. It highlights a love that sees us as who we are and love us regardless. Love planned us, developed us, and continues to want the best out of our live and for our lives. God is love, and he is true to himself. That is why he is genuine the, Real Deal Love.

Daynel W. Collins

Messed Up From

The Word Go

Daynel W. Collins

Messed Up From the Word Go.

This second chapter talks about rocky or imperfect foundations. It discusses what to do when your traditions are tragic. When childhood and family lives are messed up. When are starting points hinder us rather than help us. When questions leave us stalled at the

starting point; and, were just Messed Up From
The Word Go.

These are the many ways that I have heard
males talk about being raised in a single parent
home run by women. Your statements lie in
two major areas your manhood and fatherhood.
You feel that you do not have a standard of
measurement or system of judgment to go by.
Due to your father's departure, you feel that
you need to figure these things out alone.
However, what makes you good or even great in
both of these areas is not modeling after any
parent male or female. It is modeling after God
who they are supposes to be training you to be

like. Being a humble and obedient parent unto Christ is one of the hardest things that a man or a woman may face. Parents sometimes get lost in teaching about family legacy, teaching you how to be successful in society and things that seem proper. However in the bible it discusses that we should watch teaching legacy and a reliance on the worlds system. In 1 Timothy 1:4 AMP, "Nor to give importance to or occupy themselves with legends (fables, myths) and endless genealogies, which foster and promote useless speculations and questionings rather than acceptance in faith of God's administration and the divine training that is in faith (in that

51

Daynel W. Collins

leaning of the entire human personality on God in absolute trust and confidence)". This scripture warns parents or any teachers to teach about God not heritage or a reliance on any thing other than God. Like good or bad sayings that are not scriptural, teaching reliance on heritage to promote strength and or faith in ones self and not the Lord. A parent's first priority is teaching that God is enough and they are direct descendant of him. They are children of The Most High God that makes them a prince or princess of God. This is the duty of all Christian parents to help them realize who they are in Christ. To train them to be spiritual mature. Not, to make them successful in life, to develop their self-esteem, or help them find out were they originate from on earth. Many men in our churches, homes, and workplace all over our society are grown, grown boys not grown men. You are functioning adults maintaining jobs, taking care of finances, communicating on an adult level but spiritual not mature. A parent job is to help develop a child into God's image. To be a man or a woman is to be like the image that you were created to be. In the bible, it talks about your image and the benefits of this image. It is written in Genesis 1:26KJV "And God said, Let us make man in our image, after our likeness: and let them have dominion over the fish of the sea, and over the fowl of the air, and over the cattle, and over all the earth, and over every creeping thing that creepeth upon the earth." This scripture is saying to be a man you must be what God has designed you to be. Then it goes on to the benefits of being this man talking about dominating or having control of your environment and your life. Succeeding and doing well in the areas where God has placed you. When you stay focused on him if the image of God is taught those other things will be add.

If your placement is now being a father, the answer is in your image. Since, God the father is the ultimate example of fatherhood. God's word the bible has the answer. The answer for fatherhood is found in the bible at Ephesians 6:4 AMP "Father, do not irritate and provoke your children to anger [do not exasperate them to resentment], but rear them [tenderly] in the training and discipline and the counsel and admonition of the Lord." This scripture gives a definition of how a parent is supposes to act according to his child regardless of gender. It has two main-points. The first point is emphasized. It is not to be the source of your child's anger. To be focused on keeping yourself in a place of respect, admiration and honor with your children by dong the right things. Including showing humbleness through apologizes if you have caused an offense or injured them slightly or to the point of resentment. We already know that these apologize are never too late. This point of the scripture deals with humbleness, accountability, and righteousness, over protocol and position. Which are things that are often not talked about in church along with this scripture. The second point of this scripture deals with accurate training of your children teaching and showing them repetitively and daily about God. It doesn't say sports, secular academics, church or other interests it says God specifically. In our society there is a lot of talk on education, in our churches, temples, synagogues, house of study and worship. We need to make sure we are properly educating our next generations and ourselves. We are so focused on the world system but we need to be focused on God system first. Men even if you don't have children you still need to be concerned.

This paragraph focuses on how to spread truelove and leave a legacy of that love on earth. To give truelove is to give God. Love and God are equal terms but God and the bible are also equal. The bible is God's word and God says, "he is his word." Checkout John 1:1 KJV, "In the beginning was the Word, and the Word was with God, and the Word was God." It says that God is the word, that these two concepts are the same or interchangeable. This is how truelove is spread. This is why education on love is an importance, because; without a proper education of love it is mistaken for passion filled loveless relationships. Whether they are parental, a friendship, martial and or other interpersonal relationships teaching and making sure understanding is occurring through God's word is being loving. Leaving a legacy of love is spreading the word of God. The scripture Numbers 14:18 KJV, "The Lord is longsuffering, and of great mercy, forgiving iniquity and transgression, and by no means clearing the guilty, visiting the iniquity of the fathers upon the children unto the third and fourth generation." This scripture deals with spiritual curses passed on from generation to generation. Giving the word to the next generation is the option to bless them or curse them. Not only do we have the responsibility to make sure that they get the word. We also need to make sure they have an understanding of it.

In Proverbs 4:5-7AMP, "Get skillful and godly Wisdom, get understanding (discernment, comprehension, and interpretation); do not forget and do not turn back from the words of my mouth. Forsake not [Wisdom], and she will keep, defend, and protect you; love her, and she will guard you. The beginning of Wisdom is: get Wisdom (skillful and godly Wisdom)! [For skillful and godly Wisdom is the principal thing.] And with all you have gotten, get understanding (discernment, comprehension, and interpretation)." In these three verses of scriptures it discusses why. Why it is essential to get wisdom and understanding because; it provides protection, defense and guarding if we pursue it and don't turn away. These scriptures are for everybody. However, if we are seriously concerned about our next generation we need to seriously teach, set curriculum, build scholarship programs, essay contest and other activities around the pursuit of biblically education. It is a concern in every community big or small how well our children do academically we must make sure it is also in and thorough the teaching of the bible. Men have to make sure our churches and places of worship have these policies and curriculum to help our next generation. Our children need to be protected in society today and those scriptures say that giving wisdom and understanding through the word of Christ is how it gets provided. Men this is how you leave a legacy of love. This chapter and this section on fatherhood are important because, it also gives you an opportunity to give. Which is opportunity to be blessed because what you do for others God will do for you. In Luke 6:38 ICB it is written "Give, and you will receive. You will be given much. It will be poured into your hands more than you can hold. You will be given so much that it will spill into your lap. The way you give to others is the way God will give to you." God will show himself as a father to you and teach you to be father to your children and others. To do this you must know God's word and live it yourself. Without following this training program and the techniques in Ephesians 6:4 there will continue to be problems with your children and your life in many areas. Not just little problems that affect their daily lives but major problems that effect your family generations to come. Numbers 14:18 also speaks of effects of not living according to the bible create negative situations in your life that last until someone breaks them by living according to what the bible says. That you have the power to end, change and prevent many negative cycles in your children lives and multiple generations to come. Many people have had fathers but still have had lives without the benefit of eternal life, and recognizing and enjoying love. They only had another relationship that they may or may not have enjoyed. A father or any parent without God is a parent without love. Which simple means they got caught up in a negative cycle of Number 14:18?

I can understand and relate to your feeling of abandonment. I feel messed up and often confused from these similar issues a father departure. I have also heard and seen the way people treat you when you give a voice to these feelings. When you are bold enough to voice how it is effecting your manhood and fatherhood. Since, you feel that this has stunted your spiritual and emotional growth. You wonder somehow if a man would have had a hand in raising you would things be different. For every major failure, you wonder if somehow a father could have helped. You could have produced a victory instead of a challenge without a payoff. After, your explanations, some simple say get over it other say, "excuses, excuses" others say, "don't use that as a crutch get up and do something about". This is why this chapter is so important it gives you new ideas and ways to get over it. Believing the same things and doing the same things will results in the same things. Getting new information educating your self is the key to any person's success. In Proverbs 4:7 it says, "Wisdom is the principal thing; therefore get wisdom: and with all thy getting get understanding." This scripture reminds us that getting understanding is not just important but essential. You need to understand manhood and fatherhood from God's perspective. It also means if you don't seek to know God's perspective on these subjects you will always be messed up. You will be questioning and wondering about your manhood and fatherhood for no reason. This questioning and wondering could be replaced with positive, wonderful, satisfying and enjoyable life. The only way you can move on from being messed up from the word go in your childhood. Is by educating yourself in the only blood that matters, the blood of Jesus, Christ. You need to embrace it, believe it, and be what it calls you to be a man.

Daynel W. Collins

Biblical Education:

The Power Move

Daynel W. Collins

The last chapter is <u>Biblical Education: The</u> <u>Power Move</u>. Knowing the bible for yourself reading, gaining understanding, and following through creates allows power to move through your life.

Biblical education is to understand the difference between existing and living. When we as Christians accept salvation we pass from death (existence) into life so, educating yourself in the word of God give you understanding of that along with what will come in your life. There is a major element of change in your new life which is called the Spirit of God who is named the Holy Spirit. The bible in John 3:6 AMP give a description of this life change. "What is born of [from] the flesh is flesh [of the physical is physical]; and what is born of the Spirit is Spirit." So, when you accept salvation you gain God's spirit, which is called the Holy Spirit or the Holy Ghost. The Holy Spirit has many different functions and benefits. I will not go into all of them. I will, however; talk about the function of the Holy Spirit as teacher and the nine fruits of his Spirit, which are in your new life. This chapter is on biblical education and I cannot talk about it without talking about the Holy Spirit. He is the one who allows you to gain understanding of God. The Holy Spirit is the teacher of God's word. The Bible is the book that the word of God is in so it is the book you study from. Just like in a classroom there is a teacher and a textbook, well when your Christian your teacher is the Holy Spirit who dwell inside of you and your textbook is the Holy Bible. In that Bible in 1Corithians 2:10-13 AMP it gives an in depth description of how the Holy Spirit works as our teacher teaching us about God. "Yet to us God has unveiled and revealed them by and through His Spirit, for the [Holy] Spirit searched diligently, exploring examining everything, even sounding the profound and bottomless things of God [the divine counsels and things hidden and beyond mans scrutiny]. For what person perceives (knows and understands) what passes through a man thoughts except the man's own spirit within him? Just so one discerns (comes to know and comprehends) the thoughts of God except the Spirit of God. Now we have not received the spirit [that belongs to] the world, but the [Holy] Spirit who is from God, [given to us] that we might realize and comprehend and appreciate the gifts [of divine favor and blessing so freely and lavishly] bestowed on us by God. And we are setting these truths forth in words not taught by human wisdom but taught by the [Holy] Spirit, combining and interpreting spiritual truths with spiritual language [to those who posses the Holy Spirit]." The Holy Spirit will never stop being the teacher. We must be willing to be alert and attentive students reading our bibles paying attention in church and in bible study and wherever the Bible is being taught.

Being biblically educated allows us to have more opportunity to understand our new life. This makes your life more powerful in two specific ways it prepares and allows you to have power over your enemy, just like any other education it prepares you for what is ahead in your life. If you were studying medicine it would prepare you to be a doctor. If you study communications it would prepare you to be a public speaker. Studying law prepares you to be a lawyer. It is the same with studying the bible when you educate yourself on God and who gives life. You will feel more alive and understand your life a lot better. Preparing your self in your task brings confidence, vitality, and assurance. It is because you have proper knowledge to back you up, proof. When people say that they are prepared for a task usually they are not just believed and given a job. They will have to produce proof in several different forms written proof a resume and oral proof an interview. On the resume there is proof of education and prior employment that give more proof of experience because it has description of task performed. Then you have to back up that written proof with oral proof a job interview. To see if you could accurately answer questions based on the job that is offered and the proof that is written on that resume. If you can't prove that everything that you have written down is accurate and that the education you received is enough for the position you will not get the job. If you have gotten this job and the proof that you have on your resume is false this job will be hard until you gain education need for the position. You may even lose the job in the process, because; you are not qualified to have that position. It is the same for all Christians until you have proof and understanding of your life in God. You will live miserable life or lose what is yours to keep within your life. It because you are not confident, assured and don't have the vital biblical information that biblical education can only give you. Biblical education brings preparation for life built on nine fruits of the Holy Spirit. When you build these fruits up in your life by gaining knowledge of God through the Bible it brings assurance, vitality and confidence. You will appear confident know matter what the situation. You will not be weighed down or depressed, because; you will understand who you are inside which makes your life vital. Biblical education gives assurance to your life. You will be able to use the scripture that you have learned as proof that your hard times will lead to blessings and abundance. The bible itself is that proof and the nine fruits of the Holy Spirit which dwell inside of you allows you to know this proof even when there is no other external, physical or emotional proof.

Being biblically educated is being taught the bible in its entire truth. The sermons, bible studies, biblically literature, all teaching and teaching tools need to rightly the divide the word. Give the bible and the message that it carries to represent the holiness of God. When I say holiness of God or Christ. I mean the nine fruits of the Holy Spirit which are found in Galatians 5:22. The nine fruits are love, joy, peace, patience, kindness, goodness, faithfulness, gentleness, and self-control. Pastors, teachers, biblical educators all who are Christians have a responsibility to receive and give the word in the balance of those nine fruits. Cultivating nine fruits of the Holy Spirit that make your life strong, abundant, healthy and enjoyable life. It is what makes a major difference in your life. A lot of people are Christians; however, these things are what make being a Christian worthwhile. Without biblical education you will live lives full of hellish experiences rather than joy, peace, kindness, goodness, faithfulness, patience, gentleness, love, and self-control. Throughout, the Bible in every scripture, story, character and chapter these nine fruits are represented. Every person that is in the Bible that lived a productive life these nine fruits of the Holy Spirit were represented in their life. Every time a person went through troubles, hard times or a tragic end one, several, or all these fruits were missing. So, the Bible is the tool that helps cultivate these fruits. They grow when they are nurtured through the scriptures like putting water on seeds. When these seeds are watered with scriptures they function and grow in your life.

One of the major benefits of this growth is clarity or not to be deceived. It is a great asset because, that is how or enemy works through deception. One of the nicknames for our enemy is called deceiver and that is his tragedy to rob us from abundant life on earth and in heaven. In Revelations 12:9 AMP it says, "And the huge dragon was cast down and out-that age-old serpent, who is called the Devil and Satan, he who is the seducer (deceiver) of all humanity the world over; he was forced out and down to the earth, and his angels were flung out along with him." It describes our enemies true appearance, two proper name are given for him, how he operates, and how long his been operating, and what happen to him when he decide to become the deceiver. The devil works through deception he is our only enemy. He attacks Christians by trying to make them believe that the promises of the Lord are not true and that if you sin you forfeit salvation. His tricks are not just limited to Christians he attacks non-believers as well. The trick for people who do not have salvation is that they will have to live perfectly, that God wants them to be holy or without sin so guilt is used to keep them from asking for their salvation. These are two of the oldest tricks our enemy uses to stop us from living a life God has promised us in his word. This is why studying and becoming aware of the tactics of our enemy is and the promise of our Lord is so important. Since, following through on what God tells you to do bring victories in life that cannot be stopped. Knowing, the truth about how your enemy operates really gives you power so you can move on to do what you are suppose to do with courage and boldness, which is to live and abundant life.

He wants to rob us of what God want to give us life and abundant life. We receive life through salvation. Abundant life is salvation and

Daynel W. Collins

an understanding the benefits or blessings that come with it. In John 10:10 KJV it states, "The thief cometh not, but for to steal, and to kill, and to destroy: I am come that they might have life, and that they might have it more abundantly." This scripture reveals one thing that comes through the education of the Bible. Continuing to not be educated in his word will cause your life to be stolen from you, which will lead to death and destruction. In your life as a whole and in the roles you will play if you don't prepare properly for them. Your role as father, friend, husband, employee or employer will be destroyed if you don't properly see them through the word of God. Things that are designed to prosper in your life like relationships with your families, money, health, and etc. When failures occur in these relationships it leaves us feeling lifeless and depressed. There will always be attacks in these areas but it is easier to handle with proper education of where they're coming from and information to fight them with.

The devil tries to steal deceive you out of abundant living to steal God's glory. If he can trick you into believing that reality is truth he has stolen from you, others around you and God. He deceives you when you are not educated by truth but trying to deal with the reality of life. Truth is what the bible says about a situation. Reality is how the situation actually is or appears on the physical level not on the spiritual one. For, example a person who is saved who has not cultivated any of their fruit may act mean but has fruit of goodness, mercy, kindness, love and joy. A person has the physical signs of being sick. According to the bible this person has perfect health, however; reality says that when person feels sick or shows sign of poor health they are sick. If you pull out proof of your health scriptures that say you are healthy the truth will out weigh reality. The deceiver also works in situation that we want to believe. Such as if there is nothing wrong don't fix it. For instance, sex makes you feel good. You may even be having a good committed relationship with a partner. You're a grown up and there are a grown up, you are not hurting any one and they are not hurting anyone. However, it is deception to believe that God's word is not true and you will not suffer the consequences of not being married. Marriage would be a blessing to you and it would give God glory that he deserves and any time this is not done the devil wins a battle that he is designed to lose. Due to this lost battle you will forfeit some of your abundance in life or in simpler terms give up your blessing. You have allowed yourself to be deceived by believing doing it your way is better than doing it God's way. God has plan for our life to give abundance of his self and his riches to us and to receive the glory that he deserves for himself. This will never happen if we don't educate ourselves on who we are as Christians, and the benefits we gain from being his children in truth and not in reality. God is truth and Jesus is truth. Jesus is the truth that came to this earth, died, and rose again and then sent truth back to live inside of us. The Holy Spirit is the truth that lives inside of us and teaches us what to do when reality gets raggedy. Remember, truth out weighs reality it has three people backing it up the Holy Spirit, Jesus and God. A book called the Bible and you if you decide to use it. Now, in the bible it talks about Jesus being this truth in John 14:6-7 AMP "Jesus said to him, I am the Way and the Truth and the Life; no one comes to the Father except by (through) Me. If you had know me [had learned to recognize Me], you would also have know My Father. From now on, you know Him and have seen Him." This scripture is showing proof of what I said that Jesus is truth, God is truth, and the spirit of God who is called the Holy Spirit is truth. The bible gives you and understanding of who you are being reality and truth. Flesh and spirit it allows you take hold of blessing in the spirit in bring them into reality. It gives you awareness of your enemy who is trying to stop this from happening. Who is working to deceive you in to believe that what you see is what you can get and that is all. That is why studying and operating in truth instead of reality is so important. In the bible in Proverbs 19:8 NIV it says that going after truth is how you show you love yourself "He who gets wisdom loves his

STRONG HELP FOR STRONG MEN

own soul; who cherishes understanding prospers."

Look at our society the things that we have education on are developing and growing. The things that we do not have education on are falling apart. In Hosea 4:6 AMP it says exactly why, "My people are destroyed for lack of knowledge; because you (the priestly nation) have rejected knowledge, I will also reject you that you shall be no priest to Me; seeing you have forgotten the law of your God, I will also forget your children." This scripture deals with three main issues. The first is education; second the type of education biblical and the effect of on our future. God wants us to be educated and educated in him. We go to church and church functions but we are still not educated on God. This destruction is caused because; we do not study God and what he wants for our lives. We need to be focused on educating ourselves on the bible and not religious practices. Most Christians believe that being a good church member; a nice person and the salvation will keep you from the destruction that this scripture is speaking of. Only being educated in the word and following that education through helps you escape destruction. Being a good saved church member you will miss many of your blessings.

They will be missed while you are participating in religious activities. Believing that participating you are being holy. When in fact participating alone without education and proper actions of that education you are going toward destruction for your life and your future generations. America is prime example of a nation that has rejected a biblical based society it is very religious and our children our suffering from this mistake. We see this in our communities, on television and in our own homes. We are not teaching the bible but rejecting it for religious experiences. When we go to church we are taught to be nice people and the benefit will be that good things will happen. However, people are doing just that. Still are news is filled with how our lives are growing more destructive high unholy sexual activity, violence, racism, obesity, suicide, health issues and much more. The scripture in Hosea 4:6 puts the blame at our own doorstep not at the media, the times we live in, music, videos, video games or etc. It says we must ourselves gain and not reject the knowledge of God. I am not hating on church or down playing its role.

I am just a person who grew up in them and has not seen a lot of people enjoying life, because; they still don't know God. They don't know how to cultivate those nine fruits of The Holy Spirit. Most people who go to church have salvation. However, they believe that going and being nice keeps you out of hell. This shows that we only know bits and pieces of God because church is only one format that is truly acceptable for us to enjoy him in. It is time for us to know God every day and not just once a week. It is time for us to know what we truly are. If we are Christians, we need to be studied up on Christianity. If a person calls himself or herself a doctor of cardiology, I hope, they have studied well and hard before he starts living his doctor lifestyle. It is the same for us. If we want a Christians lifestyle we have to be studied and operating in our studies. When we begin to operate in these studies we will produce a rich satisfying life. All we need to produce them is the bible the word of God because the rest has been placed in us through the Holy Spirit. I could go on non-stop and write about biblical education because it is education of life. This chapter and throughout the book I have tried to show how biblical education effects you. By, showing how the bible illustrates God as love, that God is love and that loving him has a specific format just saying it doesn't work and that nothing can be confused with love because,

God is love. I also showed that conforming to the image of God is the definition of manhood and fatherhood is teaching someone else to conform to that image is fatherhood.

I know that I have pleased God by writing this book as act of faith and obedience. I pray that you are blessed by what you have gained. In Jesus Christ name I pray that.

About the Author

Daynel W Collins

Is a young lady who has one mission in life to be obedient to God's will in her heart, soul and strength in every area of her life. Mentally, physically, spiritually and emotionally she want to carry out her gifts, talents, abilities and task for the love of God. Strong Help for Strong Men is one of those tasks and also her debut as author. She currently resides in Rochester, PA with her family consisting of her mother, sister and nephew.

www.ingramcontent.com/pod-product-compliance
Lightning Source LLC
Chambersburg PA
CBHW030339290526
45785CB00004B/1534